For my Parents
and for Nicholas, Alexander, Jérôme, Julien and Romain,
the children who are closest to me.

Kevin Kling

CHILDREN OF THE WORLD

ABRAMS, NEW YORK

Hide-and-seek, Chota Valley, Ecuador

Above: Twin wrestlers, Gobi Desert, Mongolia

Opposite page: Twins, Suzhou, China

Opposite page: Spring walk, Gobi Desert, Mongolia
Above: Schoolgirl, oasis in the Taklamakan desert, China

Following pages: Rituals at the Mahabodhi stupa, Bodhgaya, India
Blowing bubbles, China

Above: Camel herder, Mount Sinai, Egypt

Opposite page: Graduation day, Rajasthan, India

After prayer, Tashilumpo monastery, Tibet

'There's the Dalai Lama!', Kalachakra Initiation, Mongolia

Opposite page and above: Grandmothers with grandchildren, China

Grape harvest, oasis in the Tarim Basin, China

Nap time, Thailand

Exploring the Forbidden City, Beijing, China

Friends, Gansu Province, China

Banni Cradle, Great Rann of Kutch, India

Almost home, China

Above: 'Guess who?', Bodnath, Nepal

Opposite page: H'Mong acrobats, Thailand

Opposite page: Frog fishing, Thailand

Above: Girl adjusting her earring, Thailand

Africa

Meet Gesaheyn, Kaffa, Western Highlands, Ethiopia

This evening, I am invited for the traditional coffee ceremony. Maryam has arranged for her youngest son to show me the way. I find this little five-year-old Oromo boy enchanting. He is dressed like an African angel. He wears the traditional white cotton shawl, the soft, transparent *shamma*, but it is far too long and swathes him from head to toe, leaving only his face and bare feet visible. Gesaheyn and I stroll down an earthen track burnt orange by the sun. Colobus monkeys, all luminous eyes and black and white tails, swing through the trees above our heads, thrashing and cackling incessantly, as if making fun of us. Gesaheyn hardly notices. This is his world: a world of mountains, monkeys and coffee trees, their branches now full of cherry-red beans ripe for harvest. The coffee fields are now very far behind us. Gesaheyn and I continue along a narrow path through the tangled jungle. A three-quarter moon rises above the green foliage clearly visible on the daytime, blue sky. Now the path divides in two. Gesaheyn stops suddenly, smelling the air. At five, he has the reflexes of an expert tracker. His black eyes widening with thought, he gazes towards one path then arches his neck toward the other. The monkeys are laughing. Gesaheyn turns to me. He extends two of his fingers, his thumb and index, from beneath the enveloping *shamma*. Trusting him, in spite of his age, I let him decide and then follow in the direction pointed by his tiny thumb. He has chosen a shortcut; a few minutes later, we emerge from the bush to confront the awesome mountainous terrain of the Great Rift Valley. As he approaches familiar sights and the scent of home – fragrant coffee beans roasting over the fire – his small footsteps pick up speed. His long white *shamma* slips off his head and flutters behind him in the wind. Maryam awaits us.

Gesahegn

Amhara shepherd, Tisisat (Blue Nile), Ethiopia

Above: Camel fair, Rajasthan, India

Opposite page: Traditional ferris wheel, Thar Desert, India

First riding lesson, Arkhangai steppe, Mongolia

Young shepherdess, near Anye Machin, Tibet

Above: Feast of San Juan, Salasaca, Ecuador

Opposite page: Catch-me-if-you-can, Kashgar, China

Above: Baby, Thar Desert, India

Opposite page: Uighur cradle on the Silk Road, China

Opposite page: Buddhist Kalachakra Initiation, Bodhgaya, India   *Above:* Blowing bubbles, Xishuangbanna, China

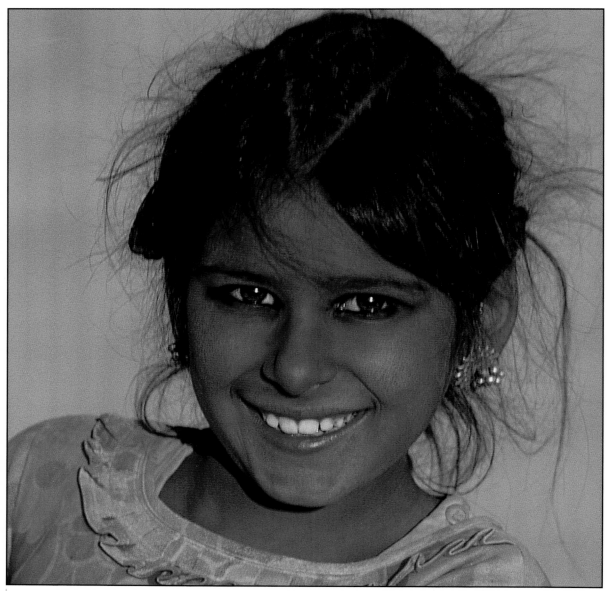

Above: Young girl, Gujarat, India   *Opposite page:* Prayers at dawn on New Year's Day, Gandan Monastery, Mongolia

*I*ndia

Meet Saurabh, Barmer district, Rajasthan

Every year, when the November moon reaches its full *(Kartik-Purnima)*, the Ribari nomads head east across the Thar Desert with their families, taking their herds of camel and zebu cattle along with them. For little Saurabh (his name means 'Fragrance'), this will be his first visit to the Camel Fair *(Mela)*. The annual gathering takes place on sandy dunes overlooking a lake sacred to the Brahmans of Rajasthan. The waters lie like a sapphire in the desert. Legend has it that it was created by Brahma from the petals of a lotus flower.

Night by night the moon swells and the clear desert skies glitter with myriad constellations. I meet Saurabh for the first time beneath the constellation Orion; he is asleep, huddled next to his parents, Gita and Mahendra. Their faces are lit by embers from the camel-dung fire. The baby boy dreams peacefully, wrapped tightly in his saffron shawl, snuggled under his mother's delicately embroidered quilt. With the hospitality shown by nomads everywhere, his parents invite me to share a plate of *dal* (lentils) and *bagri*, the local unleavened bread made from millet flour. Although Saurabh is only an infant, he is about to receive an initiation in the life of his forefathers. He will spend fourteen days and nights surrounded by the unfamiliar dunes, camping amid 5,000 other families. Due to a tough year of drought, Saurabh's father Mahendra faces harsh competition if he wants to sell his eight thin camels for a decent price. On the night of the full moon, the culmination of the *Mela*, Gita will step barefoot down the *ghat*, the narrow steps into the lake. Haloed in silvery moonlight, she will tenderly cradle her young son. Finding her balance on the *ghat*, she will make the traditional blessing *(puja)* by dipping Saurabh seven times into the holy waters.

Opposite page: Spinning cotton, India
Above: 'Namaste' (Hindu greeting), Barmer, India

Previous pages: Climbing a Ming balustrade, Kunming, China
Sisters, Tonghai, China

Opposite page: Lunch in the Summer Palace, Beijing, China
Above: Fan dance, Xian, China

Above and opposite page: Nursery school, Beijing, China

Opposite page: Grandfather's bicycle, Guilin, China
Above: In the shade of the poplar trees, Kashgar, China

Following pages: Saraguros, Sunday market, Ecuador
Learning to read, Otavalo, Ecuador

Above: Mongol winter, Zuunmod, Mongolia

Opposite page: After the funeral, Yunnan, China

Monsoon morning, Thailand

Opposite page: Kazakhs playing on the frozen river in the spring, Mongolia   *Above:* Young Mongol horse rider

| Caravan, Uvs aimag, Mongolia

Swaddled twins, Mongolia

Riding in the Tien Shan mountains, China

Young nomad, Zavhan, Mongolia

Asia

Meet Enkhbatar, Uvurkhangai aimag, Mongolia

Winter in Mongolia is at its coldest in January and February. This is the season of the Mongolian New Year: *Tsaagan Sar* (the White Month). Though the land is blanketed with snow, for Mongols white symbolises milk rather than cold. In Mongolia, the New Year is the herald of spring. Since the time of Genghis Khan, young Mongol boys and girls have tested their prowess in horsemanship on the icy ground of the White Month. This is the most difficult of all races: a twenty-five kilometre ride with the glacial air-temperature at minus thirty degrees Celsius. A Mongol mother never sends her child into the steppe without the traditional Buddhist blessings. Enkhbatar's mother, Altangul, emerges from her *ger* (tent-house) with a pail of milk and a spoon. She dips the spoon four times, flicking the milk to the four points of the compass. Jaargal, his father, sprinkles the ears and rump of the horse, then gives the rest of the milk to his son to drink. An adept of these races since the age of five, Enkhbatar is well aware of the tough ride that lies ahead and of the stiff competition. He knows from experience to rein his horse in till he joins the others at the starting line. Only Mongols have the stamina for such a competition; this tradition has been passed down from generation to generation. For Mongol children, this is a coming-of-age rite. On this frozen wintry morning, more than fifty children gallop flat out across the snowy earth. The horses snort and cavort, their breath steaming. Frost clings to their lashes and nostrils. Freezing sweat makes their fur a crusty coat of ice. The children give the traditional Naadam yodel as they charge. At the start they are neck and neck, but the older riders, the eleven- to fourteen-year-olds, are handicapped by their weight; their horses tire more quickly and fall behind. Nine-year-old Ulzii wins in the end, but Enkhbatar says that his hopes are still high; for after all, next year, the Year of the Rooster, victory will be his!

Enkhbatar

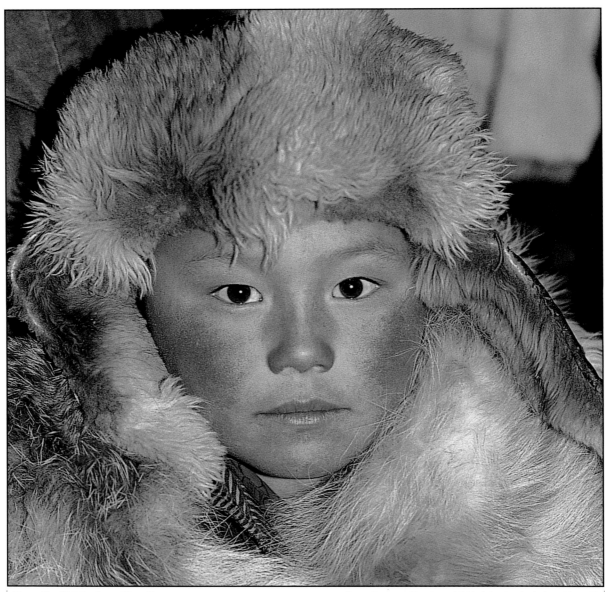

Above: Kazakh lute player, Mongolia   *Opposite page:* Tsaatane child helping tend reindeer, Mongolia

Shepherd, Bale Mountains, Ethiopia

Shepherd, Andes, Peru

Newar girl carrying water, Nepal

Nyemo girl, Tibet

On the way to the Jokhang Temple, Lhasa, Tibet

Kazakh, Tien Shan mountains, China

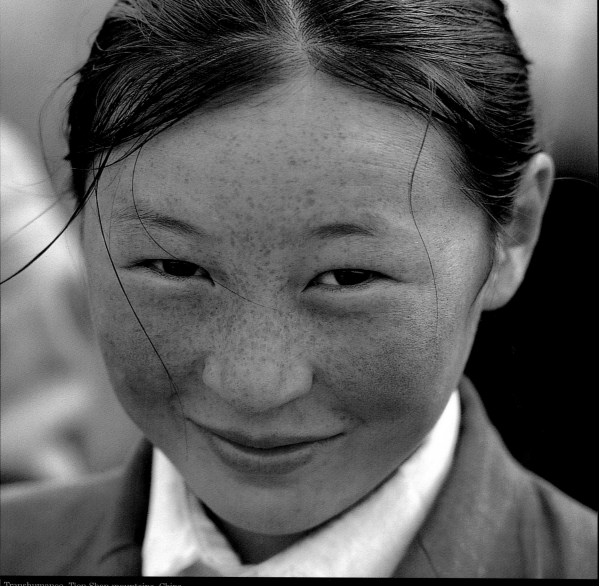
Transhumance, Tien Shan mountains, China

Above: Llama shepherdess, Altiplano, Peru

Opposite page: Children fishing, Lake Titicaca, Peru

Opposite page: Girl carrying mare's milk, Altai Mountains, Mongolia

Above: Gobi desert, Mongolia

Above: Discovering lotus flowers, Summer Palace, Beijing, China   *Opposite page:* Wild flowers in the summer, Ecuador

Summer solstice festival, Zuleta, Ecuador

Shepherdess on the volcanic slopes, Andes, Ecuador

Above and opposite page: May, Altai Mountains, Mongolia

Amhara girl, plateau of the Great Rift Valley, Ethiopia

Sahara shepherdess, Morocco

Africa

Meet Amba, Lalibela, Ethiopia

It is the afternoon of Saturday, 22 February, and market day in Lalibela, the jewel in the Ethiopian crown. But it is not just any market day on the high plateau. This is the last Saturday one can eat meat for one month. The Easter fast will soon begin for Amba as for everyone of the Coptic faith (a branch of Christianity). Perhaps it is a good omen to meet this Amhara beauty at such a holy time. She is fifteen years old and is to be married to a man twenty-three years her senior. It is common for Amhara girls to marry during adolescence. Easter coincides with the 'wedding season', a time when the days are warm and dry even on the high plateau. A musician plays the masenko, a one-stringed fiddle, while Amba's mother sings traditional improvised love songs. Amba, whose chiselled face resembles that of a Biblical princess, dances with her cousins. As the girls clap out the rhythm, they move together in a circle, taking turns to toss the *injira*, spongy pancakes made out of teff-flour, cooking on the flat, black pans over the courtyard fire. Others stir the *wat*, a spicy goat stew, the last they will taste before the end of Lent. Tonight Amba will spend one final night with her family in the thatch-roofed *tukul* where she was born. It stands a little way up the mountain from St. Giorgis, one of the most sacred of the fabled rock-cut churches of Lalibela. As tradition requires, Asafa, her husband-to-be, will fetch her on horseback at the crack of dawn.

Opposite page: Girl carrying camel's milk, Brava, Somalia

Above: Oromo shepherdess, Asela, Ethiopia

Above: Nomad girl, summer, Kham, Tibet

Opposite page: Milking yaks, Mongolia

Above: Young Uighur, Altyn Tagh oasis, China
Opposite page: Yao games, Thailand

Above and opposite page: Daily life, Silk Road, China

Teatime, oasis in the Tarim basin, China

'My little brother', Xinjiang Province, China

Heart-to-heart, Pujili, Ecuador

Puruhua baby with mother, Chimborazo Province, Ecuad

On dad's feet, Gujarat, India

Desert girl, Great Rann of Kutch, India

Opposite page: Yuanyang children, China   *Above:* Baby, Ailao Shan, China

Whispering Wall, Forbidden City, Beijing, China

Afternoon in the shade, Turfan oasis, China

$\mathcal{S}$outh $\mathcal{A}$merica

Meet Sholita, Chimborazo Province, Ecuador

Along the "Avenue of the Volcanoes" on the Equatorial line, climate is determined by altitude. In the Andes, high above the banana plantations of the Oriente or the jungle of the Amazon basin, animal husbandry is the only livelihood. Here, as in most mountainous regions, it is the children who tend the flocks. At the bottom of snow-laden summits, they herd llamas, sheep or cows. Sholita runs along the sunken dust-path, which is bordered by maguey cactus. At the end of the day, she must gather her herd more quickly than other shepherds at higher latitudes. Near the equator, days and nights are of equal length and night falls fast. All the sheep must be safely inside their pen before six in the evening if they are not to stray in the dark. If they did, they would be impossible to find unless the moon were full. Dusk is falling.

Sholita's faded pink poncho flutters as the evening winds pick up. Temperatures drop abruptly as the sun disappears behind the crests. Little Sholita chases her sheep up and down the slope in the direction of her thatch-roofed *choza*. As she runs, she keeps an eye on her *taita*, her 'father' in Quechua, the language she inherited from her Inca ancestors. 'Father Chimborazo' is not her real father, but instead the second highest volcano in the Andes. The Puruhua Indians, who live in its shadow, revere this peak and always refer affectionately to 'Taita Chimborazo' as their 'great white protector'.

Today is the Feast of San Juan, the festival of the summer solstice. In the tradition of Sholita's forefathers, 'Inti', the sun, will be honoured with chalango music and a special menu: potatoes the size of chickpeas and guinea pig soup. *Chicha*, beer made from cactus, will flow freely, however, only for the elders.

Sholita

| *Above:* Looking after the fawn, Hovsgol Taiga, Mongolia

Opposite page: Apprentice eagle hunter, Mongolia |

Above: Swaddled in baby-carrier, Uvs aimag, Mongolia

Opposite page: Kazakh girl with her lamb, Mongolia

Thank you

I would like to thank the following people with all my heart for their help in bringing this book into existence: Hervé de la Martinière, Brigitte Govignon, Audrey Demarre, Eugénie Rambaud, Rémi Coignet, Brigitte Françoise, Sophie Giraud, Marianne Lassandro, Margaret Buchanan, Marie-Laure Garello and everyone else at La Martinière Groupe. A special appreciation to Ochirbal who created the design of my stamp which I use as my signature.

I would also like to thank all those who have encouraged me in my photographic projects around the theme 'Children of the World'. At the Sénat: Alain Delcamp, Alain Méar, François Wicker, Jean-Michel Houlbert, Olivier Josse; at UNICEF France: Jacques Hintzy and Yasmine Hamdi; at the Photo Laboratory, Pictorial Service: the late Eddy Gassmann, Paulette, Patricia, Philippe Gassmann and Ricardo Moreno; at Linklaters: Nathalie Hobbs, Anne-Claire Morillon, for her constant help, Patricia Peterson, Arnaud Theulier Saint-Germain Florent Gouverneur, Guillaume Knerr, Audrey Durepaire and Evelyne Second for their support and advice; and my beloved husband, Paul Tapponnier.

Most of all I wish to thank and honour all the children I have had the good fortune to cross paths with during the last twenty-five cycles of seasons of travelling through mountains and deserts and across the seven seas.

British Library Cataloguing in Publication Data
A catalogue record for this book is available from the British Library.

ISBN 0–8109–7758-3

Copyright © 2006 Éditions de La Martinière, Paris
Originally published in French as *Terre d'Enfance* by
Éditions de la Martinière.

Layout and project management for the English edition:
Birgitte Juul Christensen, Dania D'Eramo, Emanuela Canclini

Printed and bound in France
10 9 8 7 6 5 4 3 2 1

HNA
harry n. abrams, inc.
a subsidiary of La Martinière Groupe